D. Mae Ward
Savannah, Georgia
31401

BUTTERFLIES AND FLOWERS
COLORING BOOK

D MAE WARD
Savannah, GA.

BUTTERFLIES AND FLOWERS COLORING BOOK

I AM DEDICATING THIS BOOK
TO MY GRANDMOTHER

BA MAMA

WHO LOVED ALL KIND
OF FLOWERS

Table of Contents

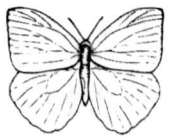

(END) "35"

www.ingramcontent.com/pod-product-compliance
Lightning Source LLC
Chambersburg PA
CBHW071308280526
45788CB00004B/1859